I0053315

The Maryland Rules of Evidence

As Approved by the
Supreme Court of Maryland

2024

MSBA
MARYLAND STATE
BAR ASSOCIATION

The Maryland State Bar Association, Inc.
Maryland Bar Center, 520 W. Fayette Street
Baltimore, Maryland 21201
(410) 685-7878

Thurgood Marshall Law Library Cataloging-in-Publication Data

Names: Maryland. Supreme Court. | Maryland State Bar
    Association.
Title: Maryland rules of evidence : as approved by the Supreme
    Court of Maryland.
Description: Pocket edition. | Baltimore, Md. : MSBA, 2024.
Subjects: Evidence (Law)—Maryland. | Court rules—Maryland. |
    Civil procedure—Maryland.
Classification: LCC KFM1740.M38 2024

ISBN: 978-1-960444-32-5

Maryland Rules
Title 5. Evidence

CHAPTER 100
GENERAL PROVISIONS

CHAPTER 200
JUDICIAL NOTICE

CHAPTER 300
PRESUMPTIONS IN CIVIL ACTIONS

CHAPTER 400
RELEVANCY AND ITS LIMITS

CHAPTER 600
WITNESSES

CHAPTER 700
OPINIONS AND EXPERT TESTIMONY

CHAPTER 800
HEARSAY

CHAPTER 900
AUTHENTICATION AND IDENTIFICATION

CHAPTER 1000
CONTENTS OF WRITINGS, RECORDINGS, AND PHOTOGRAPHS

MARYLAND RULES
TITLE 5. EVIDENCE

CHAPTER 100
GENERAL PROVISIONS

RULE 5-101

SCOPE

Effective: January 1, 2022

(a) Generally. Except as otherwise provided by statute or rule, the rules in this Title apply to all actions and proceedings in the courts of this State.

(b) Rules Inapplicable. The rules in this Title other than those relating to the competency of witnesses do not apply to the following proceedings:

    (1)   Proceedings before grand juries;

    (2)   Proceedings for extradition or rendition;

    (3)   Direct contempt proceedings in which the court may act summarily;

    (4)   Small claim actions under Rule 3-701 and appeals under Rule 7-112 (d)(2);

    (5)   Issuance of a summons or warrant under Rule 4-212;

    (6)   Pretrial release under Rule 4-216, 4-216.1, 4-216.2, or 4-216.3 or release after conviction under Rule 4-349;

    (7)   Preliminary hearings under Rule 4-221;

    (8)   Post-sentencing procedures under Rule 4-340;

    (9)   Sentencing under Rule 4-342;

    (10)   Issuance of a search warrant under Rule 4-601;

    (11)   Detention and shelter care hearings under Title 11, Chapters 200 and 400;

    (12)   Emergency hearing proceedings following the removal of a child from a court-ordered placement under Title 11, Chapters 200 and 300;

    (13)   Guardianship review hearings under Rule 11-316; and

    (14)   Any other proceeding in which, prior to the adoption of the rules in this Title, the court was traditionally not bound by the common-law rules of evidence.

(c) Discretionary Application. In the following proceedings, the court, in the interest of justice, may decline to require strict application of the rules in this Title other than those relating to the competency of witnesses:

    (1)   The determination of questions of fact preliminary to admissibility of evidence when the issue is to be determined by the court under Rule 5-104 (a);

    (2)   Proceedings for revocation of probation under Rule 4-347;

    (3)   Hearings on petitions for post-conviction relief under Rule 4-406;

(4)   Plenary proceedings in the Orphans' Court under Rule 6-462;

(5)   Proceedings under Title 11 of these Rules except proceedings listed in section (b) of this Rule and proceedings listed in Rule 11-101 (b)(2) in which strict application of the Rules in this Title is required;

(6)   Catastrophic health emergency proceedings under Title 15, Chapter 1100; and

(7)   Hearings on petitions for coram nobis under Rule 15-1206; and

(8)   Any other proceeding in which, prior to the adoption of the rules in this Title, the court was authorized to decline to apply the common-law rules of evidence.

(d) Privileges. In all actions and proceedings, lawful privileges shall be respected.

♦ ♦ ♦

Source: This Rule is derived in part from Uniform Rule of Evidence 1101 and is in part new.

Credits

[Adopted Dec. 15, 1993, eff. July 1, 1994. Amended June 5, 1996, eff. Jan. 1, 1997; April 5, 2005, eff. July 1, 2005; Nov. 8, 2005, eff. Jan. 1, 2006; Dec. 4, 2007, eff. Jan. 1, 2008; June 11, 2012, eff. June 12, 2012; May 27, 2014, eff. July 1, 2014; Dec. 7, 2015, eff. Jan. 1, 2016; February 16, 2017, eff. July 1, 2017; Nov. 9, 2021, eff. Jan. 1, 2022.]

MD Rules, Rule 5-101, MD R REV Rule 5-101

Current with amendments received through December 1, 2023. Some sections may be more current, see credits for details.

RULE 5-102

PURPOSE AND CONSTRUCTION

The rules in this Title shall be construed to secure fairness in administration, eliminate unjustifiable expense and delay, and promote the growth and development of the law of evidence to the end that the truth may be ascertained and proceedings justly determined.

◆ ◆ ◆

Cross reference: Rule 1-201.

Source: This Rule is derived without substantive change from F.R.Ev. 102. Any language differences are solely for purposes of style and clarification.

Credits

[Adopted Dec. 15, 1993, eff. July 1, 1994.]

MD Rules, Rule 5-102, MD R REV Rule 5-102

Current with amendments received through December 1, 2023. Some sections may be more current, see credits for details.

RULE 5-103

RULINGS ON EVIDENCE

(a) **Effect of Erroneous Ruling.** Error may not be predicated upon a ruling that admits or excludes evidence unless the party is prejudiced by the ruling, and

(1)   *Objection.* In case the ruling is one admitting evidence, a timely objection or motion to strike appears of record, stating the specific ground of objection, if the specific ground was requested by the court or required by rule; or

(2)   *Offer of Proof.* In case the ruling is one excluding evidence, the substance of the evidence was made known to the court by offer on the record or was apparent from the context within which the evidence was offered. The court may direct the making of an offer in question and answer form.

◆ ◆ ◆

Committee note: This Rule is not intended to preclude the making of objections or offers of proof by a motion in limine. See *Prout v. State,* 311 Md. 348 (1988), for special circumstances when an offer of proof is not required after the court has made a pretrial ruling excluding evidence. This Rule is also not intended to change the existing standard for harmless error in a criminal case. *See Dorsey v. State,* 276 Md. 638 (1976).

◆ ◆ ◆

(b) Explanation of Ruling. The court may add to the ruling any statement that shows the character of the evidence, the form in which it was offered, and the objection made.

(c) Hearing of Jury. Proceedings shall be conducted, to the extent practicable, so as to prevent

inadmissible evidence from being suggested to a
jury by any means, such as making statements or
offers of proof or asking questions within the hearing of the jury.

◆ ◆ ◆

Cross reference: See Rule 4-325 regarding plain error
in jury instructions; see also Rule 8-131 regarding
scope of appellate review.

Source: This Rule is derived in part from F.R.Ev. 103.

Credits

[Adopted Dec. 15, 1993, eff. July 1, 1994.]

MD Rules, Rule 5-103, MD R REV Rule 5-103

Current with amendments received through December 1, 2023. Some sections may be more current, see
credits for details.

RULE 5-104

PRELIMINARY QUESTIONS

(a) **Questions of Admissibility Generally.** Preliminary questions concerning the qualification of a
person to be a witness, the existence of a privilege,
or the admissibility of evidence shall be determined
by the court, subject to the provisions of section
(b). In making its determination, the court may,
in the interest of justice, decline to require strict
application of the rules of evidence, except those
relating to privilege and competency of witnesses.

Committee note: See *United States v. Zolin,* 491 U.S.
554 (1989) and *Zaal v. State,* 326 Md. 54 (1992),

noting the ability of a court, upon a proper foundation, to inspect privileged material in camera.

(b) Relevance Conditioned on Fact. When the relevance of evidence depends upon the fulfillment of a condition of fact, the court shall admit it upon, or subject to, the introduction of evidence sufficient to support a finding by the trier of fact that the condition has been fulfilled.

(c) Hearing of Jury. Hearings on preliminary matters shall be conducted out of the hearing of the jury when required by rule or the interests of justice.

Cross reference: Rule 4-252.

(d) Testimony by Accused. The accused does not, by testifying upon a preliminary matter of admissibility, become subject to cross-examination as to other issues in the case.

◆ ◆ ◆

Committee note: An accused who testifies only on a preliminary matter of admissibility can be cross-examined only on that matter and as to credibility. See also Rule 5-611(b)(2).

◆ ◆ ◆

(e) Weight and Credibility. This rule does not limit the right of a party to introduce before the trier of fact evidence relevant to weight or credibility.

◆ ◆ ◆

Source: This Rule is derived from F.R.Ev. 104.

Credits

[Adopted Dec. 15, 1993, eff. July 1, 1994.]

MD Rules, Rule 5-104, MD R REV Rule 5-104

Current with amendments received through December 1, 2023. Some sections may be more current, see credits for details.

RULE 5-105

LIMITED ADMISSIBILITY

When evidence is admitted that is admissible as to one party or for one purpose but not admissible as to another party or for another purpose, the court, upon request, shall restrict the evidence to its proper scope and instruct the jury accordingly.

◆　◆　◆

Committee note: This Rule is silent on the timing of limiting instructions. Ordinarily, if requested, such instructions should be given when the evidence is received and repeated as part of the court's final instructions to the jury.

Source: This Rule is derived without substantive change from F.R.Ev. 105. Any language differences are solely for purposes of style and clarification.

Credits

[Adopted Dec. 15, 1993, eff. July 1, 1994.]

MD Rules, Rule 5-105, MD R REV Rule 5-105

Current with amendments received through December 1, 2023. Some sections may be more current, see credits for details.

RULE 5-106

REMAINDER OF OR RELATED WRITINGS OR RECORDED STATEMENTS

When part or all of a writing or recorded statement is introduced by a party, an adverse party may require the introduction at that time of any other part or any other writing or recorded statement which ought in fairness to be considered contemporaneously with it.

◆ ◆ ◆

Committee note: The change that this Rule effects in the common law is one of timing, rather than of admissibility. The Rule does not provide for the admission of otherwise inadmissible evidence, except to the extent that it is necessary, in fairness, to explain what the opposing party has elicited. In that event, a limiting instruction that the evidence was admitted not as substantive proof but as explanatory of the other evidence would be appropriate. See *Richardson v. State,* 324 Md. 611 (1991). The Rule thus provides for the alternative of an earlier admission of evidence with regard to writings or recorded statements than does the common law rule of completeness. The timing under the common law remains applicable to oral statements and also remains as an alternative with regard to writings and recorded statements.

Cross reference: Rules 2-419, 4-261, 5-611, and 5-1001(a).

Source: This Rule is derived without substantive change from F.R.Ev. 106. Any language differences are solely for purposes of style and clarification.

Credits

[Adopted Dec. 15, 1993, eff. July 1, 1994.]

MD Rules, Rule 5-106, MD R REV Rule 5-106

Current with amendments received through December 1, 2023. Some sections may be more current, see credits for details.

CHAPTER 200
JUDICIAL NOTICE

RULE 5-201

JUDICIAL NOTICE OF ADJUDICATIVE FACTS
Effective: April 1, 2023

(a) Scope of Rule. This Rule governs only judicial notice of adjudicative facts. Sections (d), (e), and (g) of this Rule do not apply in the Appellate Court or the Supreme Court.

(b) Kinds of Facts. A judicially noticed fact must be one not subject to reasonable dispute in that it is either (1) generally known within the territorial jurisdiction of the trial court or (2) capable of accurate and ready determination by resort to sources whose accuracy cannot reasonably be questioned.

(c) When Discretionary. A court may take judicial notice, whether requested or not.

(d) When Mandatory. A court shall take judicial notice if requested by a party and supplied with the necessary information.

(e) Opportunity to Be Heard. Upon timely request, a party is entitled to an opportunity to be heard as to the propriety of taking judicial notice and the tenor of the matter noticed. In the absence of prior notification, the request may be made after judicial notice has been taken.

(f) Time of Taking Notice. Judicial notice may be taken at any stage of the proceeding.

(g) Instructing Jury. The court shall instruct the jury to accept as conclusive any fact judicially noticed, except that in a criminal action, the court shall instruct the jury that it may, but is not required to, accept as conclusive any judicially noticed fact adverse to the accused.

◆ ◆ ◆

Committee note: This Rule does not regulate judicial notice of so-called "legislative facts" (facts pertaining to social policy and their ramifications) or of law.

Source: This Rule is derived from F.R.Ev. 201.

Credits

[Adopted Dec. 15, 1993, eff. July 1, 1994. Amended April 21, 2023, eff. *nunc pro tunc* April 1, 2023]

MD Rules, Rule 5-201, MD R REV Rule 5-201

Current with amendments received through December 1, 2023. Some sections may be more current, see credits for details.

CHAPTER 300
PRESUMPTIONS IN CIVIL ACTIONS

RULE 5-301

PRESUMPTIONS IN CIVIL ACTIONS

(a) Effect. Unless otherwise provided by statute or by these rules, in all civil actions a presumption imposes on the party against whom it is directed the burden of producing evidence to rebut the presumption. If that party introduces evidence tending to disprove the presumed fact, the presumption will retain the effect of creating a question to be decided by the trier of fact unless the court concludes that such evidence is legally insufficient or is so conclusive that it rebuts the presumption as a matter of law.

(b) Inconsistent Presumptions. If two presumptions arise which conflict with each other, the court shall apply the one that is founded upon weightier considerations of policy and logic. If the underlying considerations are of equal weight, the presumptions shall be disregarded.

◆ ◆ ◆

Committee note: Section (a) of the Rule is intended to codify the approach to presumptions explicated in *Grier v. Rosenberg*, 213 Md. 248 (1957). The treatment of presumptions under this Rule is thus distinguishable from the so-called "Thayer-Wigmore bursting bubble" approach of Federal Rule 301 and the "Morgan-Type" presumption embodied by Uniform Rule 301. This Rule applies only to rebuttable evidentiary presumptions that have the effect of shifting the burden of production. It does not apply to (1) evidence that gives rise only to a permissible inference, which has the effect only of meeting the proponent's burden of production but not shifting that burden to the opposing party, (2) irrebuttable presumptions, which are rules of substantive law, or (3) rebuttable presumptions that are merely restatements of the allocation of the ultimate burden of persuasion to the opposing party, such as the presumption of innocence in a criminal case.

Source: This Rule is derived in part from Uniform Rule of Evidence 301.

Credits

[Adopted Dec. 15, 1993, eff. July 1, 1994.]

MD Rules, Rule 5-301, MD R REV Rule 5-301

Current with amendments received through December 1, 2023. Some sections may be more current, see credits for details.

RULE 5-302

APPLICABILITY OF PRESUMPTION OF ANOTHER JURISDICTION IN CIVIL ACTIONS

If a presumption recognized by another jurisdiction is to be applied in a civil action in Maryland, that presumption shall have the same effect in Maryland as it has in the other jurisdiction.

◆ ◆ ◆

Cross reference: Code, Courts Article, §§ 10-501 through 10-504.

Source: This Rule is new.

Credits

[Adopted Dec. 15, 1993, eff. July 1, 1994.]

MD Rules, Rule 5-302, MD R REV Rule 5-302

Current with amendments received through December 1, 2023. Some sections may be more current, see credits for details.

CHAPTER 400
RELEVANCY AND ITS LIMITS

RULE 5-401

DEFINITION OF "RELEVANT EVIDENCE"

"Relevant evidence" means evidence having any tendency to make the existence of any fact that is of consequence to the determination of the action more probable or less probable than it would be without the evidence.

♦ ♦ ♦

Source: This Rule is derived from F.R.Ev. 401.

Credits

[Adopted Dec. 15, 1993, eff. July 1, 1994.]

MD Rules, Rule 5-401, MD R REV Rule 5-401

Current with amendments received through December 1, 2023. Some sections may be more current, see credits for details.

RULE 5-402

RELEVANT EVIDENCE GENERALLY ADMISSIBLE; IRRELEVANT EVIDENCE INADMISSIBLE

Except as otherwise provided by constitutions, statutes, or these rules, or by decisional law not inconsistent with these rules, all relevant evidence is admissible. Evidence that is not relevant is not admissible.

◆ ◆ ◆

Source: This Rule is derived from F.R.Ev. 402.

Credits

[Adopted Dec. 15, 1993, eff. July 1, 1994.]

MD Rules, Rule 5-402, MD R REV Rule 5-402

Current with amendments received through December 1, 2023. Some sections may be more current, see credits for details.

RULE 5-403

EXCLUSION OF RELEVANT EVIDENCE ON GROUNDS OF PREJUDICE, CONFUSION, OR WASTE OF TIME

Although relevant, evidence may be excluded if its probative value is substantially outweighed by the danger of unfair prejudice, confusion of the issues, or misleading the jury, or by considerations of undue delay, waste of time, or needless presentation of cumulative evidence.

◆ ◆ ◆

Source: This Rule is derived from F.R.Ev. 403.

Credits

[Adopted Dec. 15, 1993, eff. July 1, 1994.]

MD Rules, Rule 5-403, MD R REV Rule 5-403

Current with amendments received through December 1, 2023. Some sections may be more current, see credits for details.

RULE 5-404

CHARACTER EVIDENCE NOT ADMISSIBLE TO PROVE CONDUCT; EXCEPTIONS; OTHER CRIMES

(a) Character Evidence.

    (1) *Prohibited Uses.* Subject to subsections (a)(2) and (3) of this Rule, evidence of a person's character or character trait is not admissible to prove that the person acted in accordance with the character or trait on a particular occasion.

    (2) *Criminal and Delinquency Cases.* Subsection (a)(2) of this Rule applies in a criminal case and in a delinquency case. For purposes of subsection (a)(2), "accused" means a defendant in a criminal case and an individual alleged to be delinquent in an action in juvenile court, and "crime" includes a delinquent act as defined by Code, Courts Article, § 3-8A-01.

        (A) Character of Accused. An accused may offer evidence of the accused's pertinent trait of character. If the evidence is admitted, the prosecution may offer evidence to rebut it.

    (B) Character of Victim. Subject to the limitations in Rule 5-412, an accused may offer evidence of an alleged crime victim's pertinent trait of character. If the evidence is admitted, the prosecutor may offer evidence to rebut it.

    (C) Homicide Case. In a homicide case, the prosecutor may offer evidence of the alleged victim's trait of peacefulness to rebut evidence that the victim was the first aggressor.

  (3) *Character of Witness.* Evidence of the character of a witness with regard to credibility may be admitted under Rules 5-607, 5-608, and 5-609.

(b) Other Crimes, Wrongs, or Acts. Evidence of other crimes, wrongs, or other acts including delinquent acts as defined by Code, Courts Article § 3-8A-01 is not admissible to prove the character of a person in order to show action in the conformity therewith. Such evidence, however, may be admissible for other purposes, such as proof of motive, opportunity, intent, preparation, common scheme or plan, knowledge, identity, absence of mistake or accident, or in conformity with Rule 5-413.

◆ ◆ ◆

Source: This Rule is derived from F.R.Ev. 404.

Credits

[Adopted Dec. 15, 1993, eff. July 1, 1994. Amended Oct. 20, 2010, eff. Jan. 1, 2011; Nov. 1, 2012, eff. Jan. 1, 2013; May 15, 2019, eff. July 1, 2019.]

MD Rules, Rule 5-404, MD R REV Rule 5-404

Current with amendments received through December 1, 2023. Some sections may be more current, see credits for details.

RULE 5-405

METHODS OF PROVING CHARACTER

(a) Reputation or Opinion. In all cases in which evidence of character or a trait of character of a person is admissible, proof may be made by testimony as to reputation or by testimony in the form of an opinion. On cross-examination, inquiry is allowable into relevant specific instances of conduct.

(b) Specific Instances of Conduct. In cases in which character or a trait of character of a person is an essential element of a charge, claim, or defense, proof may also be made of relevant specific instances of that person's conduct.

◆ ◆ ◆

Source: This Rule is derived from F.R.Ev. 405.

Credits

[Adopted Dec. 15, 1993, eff. July 1, 1994.]

MD Rules, Rule 5-405, MD R REV Rule 5-405

Current with amendments received through December 1, 2023. Some sections may be more current, see credits for details.

RULE 5-406

HABIT; ROUTINE PRACTICE

Evidence of the habit of a person or of the routine practice of an organization is relevant to prove that the conduct of the person or organization on a particular occasion was in conformity with the habit or routine practice.

◆ ◆ ◆

Source: This Rule is derived without substantive change from F.R.Ev. 406. Any language differences are solely for purposes of style and clarification.

Credits

[Adopted Dec. 15, 1993, eff. July 1, 1994.]

MD Rules, Rule 5-406, MD R REV Rule 5-406

Current with amendments received through December 1, 2023. Some sections may be more current, see credits for details.

RULE 5-407

SUBSEQUENT REMEDIAL MEASURES

(a) **In General.** When, after an event, measures are taken which, if in effect at the time of the event, would have made the event less likely to occur, evidence of the subsequent measures is not admissible to prove negligence or culpable conduct in connection with the event.

(b) Admissibility for Other Purposes. This Rule does not require the exclusion of evidence of subsequent measures when offered for another purpose, such as (1) impeachment or (2) if controverted, ownership, control, or feasibility of precautionary measures.

◆ ◆ ◆

Source: This Rule is derived from F.R.Ev. 407.

Credits

[Adopted Dec. 15, 1993, eff. July 1, 1994. Amended Nov. 12, 2003, eff. Jan. 1, 2004.]

MD Rules, Rule 5-407, MD R REV Rule 5-407

Current with amendments received through December 1, 2023. Some sections may be more current, see credits for details.

RULE 5-408

COMPROMISE AND OFFERS TO COMPROMISE

(a) The following evidence is not admissible to prove the validity, invalidity, or amount of a civil claim in dispute:

    (1)   Furnishing or offering or promising to furnish a valuable consideration for the purpose of compromising or attempting to compromise the claim or any other claim;

    (2)   Accepting or offering to accept such consideration for that purpose; and

    (3)   Conduct or statements made in compromise negotiations or mediation.

(b) This Rule does not require the exclusion of any evidence otherwise obtained merely because it is also presented in the course of compromise negotiations or mediation.

(c) Except as otherwise provided by law, evidence of a type specified in section (a) of this Rule is not excluded under this Rule when offered for another purpose, such as proving bias or prejudice of a witness, controverting a defense of laches or limitations, establishing the existence of a "Mary Carter" agreement, or proving an effort to obstruct a criminal investigation or prosecution, but exclusion is required where the sole purpose for offering the evidence is to impeach a party by showing a prior inconsistent statement.

(d) When an act giving rise to criminal liability would also result in civil liability, evidence that would be inadmissible in a civil action is also inadmissible in a criminal action based on that act.

Cross reference: Code, Courts Article, §§ 3-2A-08 and 5-401.1.

◆ ◆ ◆

Source: This Rule is derived from F.R.Ev. 408.

Credits

[Adopted Dec. 15, 1993, eff. July 1, 1994. Amended May 9, 2000, eff. July 1, 2000.]

MD Rules, Rule 5-408, MD R REV Rule 5-408

Current with amendments received through December 1, 2023. Some sections may be more current, see credits for details.

RULE 5-409

PAYMENT OF MEDICAL AND SIMILAR EXPENSES

Evidence of furnishing, offering, or promising to pay medical, hospital, or similar expenses occasioned by an injury is not admissible to prove civil or criminal liability for the injury.

♦ ♦ ♦

Source: This Rule is derived from F.R.Ev. 409.

Credits

[Adopted Dec. 15, 1993, eff. July 1, 1994.]

MD Rules, Rule 5-409, MD R REV Rule 5-409

Current with amendments received through December 1, 2023. Some sections may be more current, see credits for details.

RULE 5-410

INADMISSIBILITY OF PLEAS, PLEA DISCUSSIONS, AND RELATED STATEMENTS

(a) Generally. Except as otherwise provided in this Rule, evidence of the following is not admissible against the defendant who made the plea or was a participant in the plea discussions:

    (1) a plea of guilty which was not accepted or which was later withdrawn or vacated;

(2)   a plea of nolo contendere, except as otherwise provided in these rules;

(3)   any statement made in the course of any proceedings under Rule 4-243 or comparable state or federal procedure regarding a plea specified in subsection (a)(1) or (a)(2) of this Rule, except in a criminal proceeding for perjury or false statement if the statement was made by the defendant under oath and on the record; or

(4)   any statement made in the course of plea discussions with an attorney for the prosecuting authority which do not result in a plea of guilty or nolo contendere or which result in a plea of guilty or nolo contendere which was not accepted or was later withdrawn or vacated.

(b) Exceptions.

(1)   A statement of a type specified in subsections (a)(3) or (a)(4) of this Rule is not excluded under this Rule in any proceeding wherein another statement made in the course of the same plea or plea discussions has been introduced and the statement ought in fairness be considered with it;

(2)   A statement of the type specified in subsection (a)(3) of this Rule may be admissible in a subsequent civil proceeding as a prior inconsistent statement, if offered to attack

the credibility of the person who made the statement.

(c) Definition. For purposes of this Rule, a guilty plea that is the subject of an appeal from the District Court to the circuit court is not considered withdrawn or vacated.

◆ ◆ ◆

Cross reference: Rule 19-737 (g).

Source: This Rule is derived from F.R.Ev. 410.

Credits

[Adopted Dec. 15, 1993, eff. July 1, 1994. Amended June 5, 1996, eff. Jan. 1, 1997; June 6, 2016, eff. July 1, 2016.]

MD Rules, Rule 5-410, MD R REV Rule 5-410

Current with amendments received through December 1, 2023. Some sections may be more current, see credits for details.

RULE 5-411

LIABILITY INSURANCE

Evidence that a person was or was not insured against liability is not admissible upon the issue whether the person acted negligently or otherwise wrongfully. This Rule does not require the exclusion of evidence of insurance against liability when offered for another purpose, such as proof of agency, ownership, or control, or bias or prejudice of a witness.

◆ ◆ ◆

Source: This Rule is derived from F.R.Ev. 411.

Credits

[Adopted Dec. 15, 1993, eff. July 1, 1994.]

MD Rules, Rule 5-411, MD R REV Rule 5-411

Current with amendments received through December 1, 2023. Some sections may be more current, see credits for details.

RULE 5-412

SEX OFFENSE CASES; RELEVANCE OF VICTIM'S PAST BEHAVIOR

In prosecutions for any sex offense under Code, Criminal Law Article, Title 3, Subtitle 3 or a lesser included crime; the sexual abuse of a minor under Code, Criminal Law Article, § 3-602 or a lesser included crime; or the sexual abuse of a vulnerable adult under Code, Criminal Law Article, § 3-604 or a lesser included crime, admissibility of evidence relating to the victim's sexual history is governed by Code, Criminal Law Article, § 3-319.

◆ ◆ ◆

Source: This Rule is new.

Credits

[Adopted Dec. 15, 1993, eff. July 1, 1994. Amended June 8, 1998, eff. Oct. 1, 1998; Oct. 31, 2002, eff. Jan. 1, 2003; Nov. 12, 2003, eff. Jan. 1, 2004.]

MD Rules, Rule 5-412, MD R REV Rule 5-412

Current with amendments received through December 1, 2023. Some sections may be more current, see credits for details.

RULE 5-413

SEX OFFENSE CASES; OTHER SEXUALLY ASSAULTIVE BEHAVIOR BY DEFENDANT

In prosecutions for sexually assaultive behavior as defined in Code, Courts Article, § 10-923(a), evidence of other sexually assaultive behavior by the defendant occurring before or after the offense for which the defendant is on trial may be admitted in accordance with § 10-923.

◆ ◆ ◆

Cross reference: See Rule 4-251(b)(4), concerning the time for determination of a motion in the District Court.

Source: This Rule is new.

Credits

[Adopted May 15, 2019, eff. July 1, 2019.]

MD Rules, Rule 5-413, MD R REV Rule 5-413

Current with amendments received through December 1, 2023. Some sections may be more current, see credits for details.

T. 5, CH. 500, REFS & ANNOS

<THERE IS NO CHAPTER 500.>

MD Rules, T. 5, Ch. 500, Refs & Annos, MD R REV T. 5, Ch. 500, Refs & Annos

Current with amendments received through December 1, 2023. Some sections may be more current, see credits for details.

CHAPTER 600
WITNESSES

RULE 5-601

GENERAL RULE OF COMPETENCY

Except as otherwise provided by law, every person is competent to be a witness.

◆ ◆ ◆

Committee note: Under this Rule, a witness is not generally incompetent by virtue of status. A court could find, however, that because of insufficient memory, intelligence, or ability to express oneself, or inability to appreciate the need to tell the truth, a particular witness is not competent to testify as to certain matters. See Rules 5-401 through 5-403, and 5-603.

Cross reference: Code, Courts Article, §§ 9-104 and 9-116.

Source: This Rule is derived from F.R.Ev. 601.

Credits

[Adopted Dec. 15, 1993, eff. July 1, 1994.]

MD Rules, Rule 5-601, MD R REV Rule 5-601

Current with amendments received through December 1, 2023. Some sections may be more current, see credits for details.

RULE 5-602

LACK OF PERSONAL KNOWLEDGE

Except as otherwise provided by Rule 5-703, a witness may not testify to a matter unless evidence is introduced sufficient to support a finding that the witness has personal knowledge of the matter. Evidence to prove personal knowledge may, but need not, consist of the witness's own testimony.

◆ ◆ ◆

Committee note: This Rule does not prevent the admission of testimony as to a witness's own age, date of birth, or other similar matters of personal history, when a requirement of first-hand knowledge cannot be met.

Source: This Rule is derived without substantive change from F.R.Ev. 602. Any language differences are solely for purposes of style and clarification.

Credits

[Adopted Dec. 15, 1993, eff. July 1, 1994.]

MD Rules, Rule 5-602, MD R REV Rule 5-602

Current with amendments received through December 1, 2023. Some sections may be more current, see credits for details.

RULE 5-603

OATH OR AFFIRMATION

Effective: August 1, 2020

Before testifying, a witness shall be required to declare that the witness will testify truthfully. The declaration shall be by oath or affirmation administered either in the form specified by Rule 1-303 or, in special circumstances, in some other form of oath or affirmation calculated to impress upon the witness the duty to tell the truth.

◆ ◆ ◆

Committee note: In special circumstances where diminished capacity may be a concern, such as when a child or person with limited cognitive ability is called to testify, the trial court may deviate from the form of oath specified by Rule 1-303. Before administering the oath, the trial court first must find that the individual with diminished capacity is competent to testify, based upon the four essential requirements set forth in *Perry v. State*, 381 Md. 138, 149 (2004): "(1) capacity for observation; (2) capacity for recollection; (3) capacity for communication, including ability 'to understand questions put and to frame and express intelligent answers;' and, (4) a sense of moral responsibility to tell the truth" (citing 2 Wigmore, Evidence § 506 (Chadbourn rev. 1979)).

Cross reference: For the oath made by a court interpreter, see Rule 1-333 (c)(3). For the general rule of competency, see Rule 5-601. For an attorney's responsibilities concerning a client's diminished capacity, see Rule 19-301.14.

Source: This Rule is derived from former F.R.Ev. Rule 603.

Credits

[Adopted Dec. 15, 1993, eff. July 1, 1994. Amended June 29, 2020, eff. Aug. 1, 2020.]

MD Rules, Rule 5-603, MD R REV Rule 5-603

Current with amendments received through December 1, 2023. Some sections may be more current, see credits for details.

RULE 5-604

RESCINDED OCT. 31, 2002, EFF. JAN. 1, 2003

MD Rules, Rule 5-604, MD R REV Rule 5-604

Current with amendments received through December 1, 2023. Some sections may be more current, see credits for details.

RULE 5-605

COMPETENCY OF JUDGE AS WITNESS

The judge presiding at the trial may not testify in that trial as a witness. No objection need be made in order to preserve the point.

◆ ◆ ◆

Cross reference: See Rule 18-102.11 (a)(1) and (a)(2)(D).

Source: This Rule is derived from F.R.Ev. 605.

Credits

[Adopted Dec. 15, 1993, eff. July 1, 1994. Amended Dec. 2, 2004, eff. July 1, 2005; June 7, 2011, eff. July 1, 2011; June 6, 2015, eff. July 1, 2016.]

MD Rules, Rule 5-605, MD R REV Rule 5-605

Current with amendments received through December 1, 2023. Some sections may be more current, see credits for details.

(1) the conviction has been reversed or vacated;

(2) the conviction has been the subject of a pardon; or

(3) an appeal or application for leave to appeal from the judgment of conviction is pending, or the time for noting an appeal or filing an application for leave to appeal has not expired.

(d) Effect of Plea of Nolo Contendere. For purposes of this Rule, "conviction" includes a plea of nolo contendere followed by a sentence, whether or not the sentence is suspended.

◆ ◆ ◆

Committee note: See Code, Courts Article, § 3-8A-23 for the effect of juvenile adjudications and for restrictions on their admissibility as evidence generally. Evidence of these adjudications may be admissible under the Confrontation Clause to show bias; see Davis v. Alaska, 415 U.S. 308 (1974).

Source: This Rule is derived from F.R.Ev. 609 and Rule 1-502.

Credits

[Adopted Dec. 15, 1993, eff. July 1, 1994. Amended Dec. 4, 2007, eff. Jan. 1, 2008; Dec. 13, 2016, eff. Apr. 1, 2017.]

MD Rules, Rule 5-609, MD R REV Rule 5-609

Current with amendments received through December 1, 2023. Some sections may be more current, see credits for details.

RULE 5-610

RELIGIOUS BELIEFS OR OPINIONS

Evidence of the beliefs or opinions of a witness on matters of religion is not admissible for the purpose of showing that by reason of their nature the witness's credibility is impaired or enhanced, except that such evidence may be admissible to show interest or bias.

◆ ◆ ◆

Source: This Rule is derived from F.R.Ev. 610 as it has been interpreted in the Advisory Committee Note to that Rule and by the Federal Courts. Cf. *United States v. Hoffman,* 806 F.2d 703 (7th Cir.1986), cert. denied, 481 U.S. 1005 (1987); *U.S. v. Teicher,* 987 F.2d 112 (2nd Cir.1993).

Credits

[Adopted Dec. 15, 1993, eff. July 1, 1994.]

MD Rules, Rule 5-610, MD R REV Rule 5-610

Current with amendments received through December 1, 2023. Some sections may be more current, see credits for details.

RULE 5-611

MODE AND ORDER OF INTERROGATION AND PRESENTATION: CONTROL BY COURT; SCOPE OF CROSS-EXAMINATION; LEADING QUESTIONS

Effective: April 1, 2022

(a) Control by Court. The court shall exercise reasonable control over the mode and order of interrogating witnesses and presenting evidence so as to

(1) make the interrogation and presentation effective for the ascertainment of the truth, (2) avoid needless consumption of time, and (3) protect witnesses from harassment or undue embarrassment.

◆ ◆ ◆

Cross reference: For the Court Dog Program, see Code, Courts Article, § 9-501.

◆ ◆ ◆

(b) Scope of Cross-Examination.

    (1) Except as provided in subsection (b)(2), cross-examination should be limited to the subject matter of the direct examination and matters affecting the credibility of the witness. Except for the cross-examination of an accused who testifies on a preliminary matter, the court may, in the exercise of discretion, permit inquiry into additional matters as if on direct examination.

    (2) An accused who testifies on a non-preliminary matter may be cross-examined on any matter relevant to any issue in the action.

(c) Leading Questions. The allowance of leading questions rests in the discretion of the trial court. Ordinarily, leading questions should not be allowed on the direct examination of a witness except as may be necessary to develop the witness's testimony. Ordinarily, leading questions should be allowed (1) on cross-examination or (2) on the direct examination of a hostile witness, an adverse party, or a witness identified with an adverse party.

◆ ◆ ◆

Source: This Rule is derived from F.R.Ev. 611.

Credits

[Adopted Dec. 15, 1993, eff. July 1, 1994. Amended March 30, 2021, eff. July 1, 2021; Feb. 9, 2022, eff. April 1, 2022.]

MD Rules, Rule 5-611, MD R REV Rule 5-611

Current with amendments received through December 1, 2023. Some sections may be more current, see credits for details.

RULE 5-612

WRITING OR OTHER ITEM USED TO REFRESH MEMORY

If, while testifying, a witness uses a writing or other item to refresh memory, any party is entitled to inspect it, to examine the witness about it, and to introduce in evidence those portions which relate to the testimony of the witness for the limited purpose of impeaching the witness as to whether the item in fact refreshes the witness's recollection.

◆ ◆ ◆

Source: This Rule is derived from F.R.Ev. 612.

Credits

[Adopted Dec. 15, 1993, eff. July 1, 1994.]

MD Rules, Rule 5-612, MD R REV Rule 5-612

Current with amendments received through December 1, 2023. Some sections may be more current, see credits for details.

RULE 5-613

PRIOR STATEMENTS OF WITNESSES

(a) Examining Witness Concerning Prior Statement.
A party examining a witness about a prior written or
oral statement made by the witness need not show it
to the witness or disclose its contents at that time, provided that before the end of the examination (1) the
statement, if written, is disclosed to the witness and
the parties, or if the statement is oral, the contents
of the statement and the circumstances under which
it was made, including the persons to whom it was
made, are disclosed to the witness and (2) the witness
is given an opportunity to explain or deny it.

**(b) Extrinsic Evidence of Prior Inconsistent State-
ment of Witness.** Unless the interests of justice
otherwise require, extrinsic evidence of a prior
inconsistent statement by a witness is not admissible under this Rule (1) until the requirements of
section (a) have been met and the witness has failed
to admit having made the statement and (2) unless
the statement concerns a non-collateral matter.

♦   ♦   ♦

Source: This Rule is derived from F.R.Ev. 613.

Credits

[Adopted Dec. 15, 1993, eff. July 1, 1994.]

MD Rules, Rule 5-613, MD R REV Rule 5-613

Current with amendments received through December 1, 2023. Some sections may be more current, see
credits for details.

RULE 5-614

CALLING AND INTERROGATION OF
WITNESS BY COURT

(a) **Calling by Court.** After giving the parties a reasonable opportunity to object outside the presence of the jury, the court, where justice so requires, may call persons as court witnesses on its own initiative or on the request of a party. All parties are entitled to cross-examine witnesses called by the court.

(b) **Interrogation by Court.** The court may interrogate any witness. In jury trials the court's questioning must be cautiously guarded so as not to comment on the evidence or convey the court's opinion of the witness's credibility.

◆ ◆ ◆

Cross reference: Rules 2-514 and 5-706.

Source: This Rule is derived from F.R.Ev. 614.

Credits

[Adopted Dec. 15, 1993, eff. July 1, 1994.]

MD Rules, Rule 5-614, MD R REV Rule 5-614

Current with amendments received through December 1, 2023. Some sections may be more current, see credits for details.

RULE 5-615

EXCLUSION OF WITNESSES
Effective: April 1, 2022

(a) **In General.** Except as provided in sections (b) and (c) of this Rule, upon the request of a party made before testimony begins, the court shall order witnesses excluded so that they cannot hear the testimony of other witnesses. When necessary for proper protection of the defendant in a criminal action, an identification witness may be excluded before the defendant appears in open court. The court may order the exclusion of a witness on its own initiative or upon the request of a party at any time. The court may continue the exclusion of a witness following the testimony of that witness if a party represents that the witness is likely to be recalled to give further testimony.

◆ ◆ ◆

Cross reference: For circumstances when the exclusion of a witness may be inappropriate, see *Tharp v. State*, 362 Md. 77 (2000).

◆ ◆ ◆

(b) Witnesses Not to Be Excluded. A court shall not exclude pursuant to this Rule

(1)   a party who is a natural person,

(2)   an officer or employee of a party that is not a natural person designated as its representative by its attorney,

(3)   an expert who is to render an opinion based on testimony given at the trial,

(4)   a person whose presence is shown by a party to be essential to the presentation of the party's cause, such as an expert necessary to advise and assist counsel, or

(5)   a victim of a crime or a delinquent act, including any representative of such a deceased or
disabled victim, to the extent required by
statute.

◆ ◆ ◆

Cross reference: Code, Courts Article, § 3-8A-13;
Criminal Procedure Article, § 11-102 and § 11-302;
Rule 4-231.

◆ ◆ ◆

(c) Permissive Non-Exclusion. The court may permit
a child witness's parents or another person having
a supportive relationship with the child to remain
in court during the child's testimony.

◆ ◆ ◆

Cross reference: For the Court Dog Program, see
Code, Courts Article, § 9-501.

◆ ◆ ◆

(d) Nondisclosure.

(1)   A party or an attorney may not disclose to a
witness excluded under this Rule the nature,
substance, or purpose of testimony, exhibits, or
other evidence introduced during the witness's
absence.

(2)   The court may, and upon request of a party
shall, order the witness and any other persons
present in the courtroom not to disclose to a
witness excluded under this Rule the nature,
substance, or purpose of testimony, exhibits, or
other evidence introduced during the witness's
absence.

(e) Exclusion of Testimony. The court may exclude all or part of the testimony of the witness who receives information in violation of this Rule.

♦   ♦   ♦

Cross reference: *McGill v. Gore Dump Trailer Leasing, Inc.*, 86 Md. App. 416 (1991).

Source: This Rule is derived from F.R.Ev. 615 and Rules 2-513, 3-513, and 4-321.

Credits

[Adopted Dec. 15, 1993, eff. July 1, 1994. Amended Jan. 20, 1999, eff. July 1, 1999; Jan. 8, 2002, eff. Feb. 1, 2002; May 8, 2007, eff. July 1, 2007; March 30, 2021, eff. July 1, 2021; Feb. 9, 2022, eff. April 1, 2022.]

MD Rules, Rule 5-615, MD R REV Rule 5-615

Current with amendments received through December 1, 2023. Some sections may be more current, see credits for details.

RULE 5-616

IMPEACHMENT AND REHABILITATION—GENERALLY

(a) Impeachment by Inquiry of the Witness. The credibility of a witness may be attacked through questions asked of the witness, including questions that are directed at:

    (1)   Proving under Rule 5-613 that the witness has made statements that are inconsistent with the witness's present testimony;

    (2)   Proving that the facts are not as testified to by the witness;

(3)   Proving that an opinion expressed by the witness is not held by the witness or is otherwise not worthy of belief;

(4)   Proving that the witness is biased, prejudiced, interested in the outcome of the proceeding, or has a motive to testify falsely;

(5)   Proving lack of personal knowledge or weaknesses in the capacity of the witness to perceive, remember, or communicate; or

(6)   Proving the character of the witness for untruthfulness by (i) establishing prior bad acts as permitted under Rule 5-608(b) or (ii) establishing prior convictions as permitted under Rule 5-609.

(b) Extrinsic Impeaching Evidence.

(1)   Extrinsic evidence of prior inconsistent statements may be admitted as provided in Rule 5-613(b).

(2)   Other extrinsic evidence contradicting a witness's testimony ordinarily may be admitted only on non-collateral matters. In the court's discretion, however, extrinsic evidence may be admitted on collateral matters.

(3)   Extrinsic evidence of bias, prejudice, interest, or other motive to testify falsely may be admitted whether or not the witness has been examined about the impeaching fact and has failed to admit it.

(4)   Extrinsic evidence of a witness's lack of personal knowledge or weaknesses in the capacity of the witness to perceive, remember, or communicate may be admitted if the witness has been examined about the impeaching fact and has failed to admit it, or as otherwise required by the interests of justice.

(5)   Extrinsic evidence of the character of a witness for untruthfulness may be admitted as provided in Rule 5-608.

(6)   Extrinsic evidence of prior convictions may be admitted as provided by Rule 5-609.

(7)   Extrinsic evidence may be admitted to show that prior consistent statements offered under subsection (c)(2) of this Rule were not made.

(c) Rehabilitation. A witness whose credibility has been attacked may be rehabilitated by:

(1)   Permitting the witness to deny or explain impeaching facts, except that a witness who has been impeached by prior conviction may not deny guilt of the earlier crime;

(2)   Except as provided by statute, evidence of the witness's prior statements that are consistent with the witness's present testimony, when their having been made detracts from the impeachment;

(3)   Evidence through other witnesses of the impeached witness's character for truthfulness, as provided in Rule 5-608(a); or

(4)   Other evidence that the court finds relevant for the purpose of rehabilitation.

♦ ♦ ♦

Committee note: This Rule is intended to illustrate the most frequently used methods of impeachment and rehabilitation. It is not intended to be exhaustive or to foreclose other legitimate methods.

Source: This Rule is new.

Credits

[Adopted Dec. 15, 1993, eff. July 1, 1994.]

MD Rules, Rule 5-616, MD R REV Rule 5-616

Current with amendments received through December 1, 2023. Some sections may be more current, see credits for details.

RULE 5-617

Pretrial Eyewitness Identification Evidence
Effective: July 1, 2021

(a) Applicability. This Rule applies to evidence of an eyewitness identification obtained pretrial with the participation by personnel from a law enforcement agency that is offered over objection in a criminal case. Upon request of a party, this Rule may be applied in a civil case if relevant and appropriate to do so.

(b) Code Requirements. In determining whether eyewitness identification evidence is admissible, the court shall consider whether there was compliance

RULE 5-704

OPINION ON ULTIMATE ISSUE

(a) In General. Except as provided in section (b) of this Rule, testimony in the form of an opinion or inference otherwise admissible is not objectionable merely because it embraces an ultimate issue to be decided by the trier of fact.

(b) Opinion on Mental State or Condition. An expert witness testifying with respect to the mental state or condition of a defendant in a criminal case may not state an opinion or inference as to whether the defendant had a mental state or condition constituting an element of the crime charged. That issue is for the trier of fact alone. This exception does not apply to an ultimate issue of criminal responsibility.

◆　◆　◆

Committee note: Section (b) of this Rule is substantively different than F.R.Ev. 704(b). The Federal provision precludes an opinion on the ultimate issue of criminal responsibility, i.e., sanity. The Maryland Rule does not preclude such an opinion. It does, however, preclude an opinion as to whether the defendant had a required intent or mental state where that intent or state is an element of the offense. See *Hartless v. State,* 327 Md. 558 (1992).

Source: Section (a) of this Rule is derived from F.R.Ev. 704(a). Section (b) is new.

Credits

[Adopted Dec. 15, 1993, eff. July 1, 1994. Amended June 21, 1995, eff. Sept. 1, 1995.]

MD Rules, Rule 5-704, MD R REV Rule 5-704

Current with amendments received through December 1, 2023. Some sections may be more current, see credits for details.

RULE 5-705

DISCLOSURE OF FACTS OR DATA UNDERLYING EXPERT OPINION

Unless the court requires otherwise, the expert may testify in terms of opinion or inference and give reasons therefor without first testifying to the underlying facts or data. The expert may in any event be required to disclose the underlying facts or data on cross-examination.

◆ ◆ ◆

Cross reference: Rules 5-611(a) and 5-703.

Source: This Rule is derived without substantive change from F.R.Ev. 705. Any language differences are solely for purposes of style and clarification.

Credits

[Adopted Dec. 15, 1993, eff. July 1, 1994.]

MD Rules, Rule 5-705, MD R REV Rule 5-705

Current with amendments received through December 1, 2023. Some sections may be more current, see credits for details.

RULE 5-706

COURT APPOINTED EXPERTS

(a) Appointment. The court, on its own initiative or on the motion of any party, may enter an order to show cause why expert witnesses should not be appointed, and may request the parties to submit nominations. The court may appoint any expert witnesses agreed upon by the parties, and may appoint expert witnesses of its own selection. An expert witness shall not be appointed by the court unless the witness consents to act. A witness so appointed shall be informed of the witness's duties by the court in writing, a copy of which shall be filed with the clerk, or at a conference in which the parties shall have opportunity to participate. A witness so appointed shall advise the parties of the witness's findings, if any; the witness's deposition may be taken by any party. The witness shall be subject to cross-examination by each party, including a party calling the witness.

(b) Compensation. Expert witnesses so appointed are entitled to reasonable compensation in whatever sum the court may allow. The compensation thus fixed is payable from funds which may be provided by law in civil actions, proceedings involving just compensation for the taking of property, and criminal actions. In other civil actions the compensation shall be paid by the parties in such proportion and at such time as the court directs, and thereafter charged in like manner as other costs.

(c) Disclosure of Appointment. In the exercise of its discretion, the court may authorize disclosure to the jury of the fact that the court appointed the expert witness.

(d) Parties' Experts of Own Selection. Nothing in this Rule limits the parties in calling expert witnesses of their own selection.

♦ ♦ ♦

Cross reference: Rule 2-603. See Code, Courts Article, § 3-2A-09 concerning court-appointed experts in health care malpractice cases.

Source: This Rule is derived without substantive change from F.R.Ev. 706. Any language differences are solely for purposes of style and clarification.

Credits

[Adopted Dec. 15, 1993, eff. July 1, 1994. Amended Nov. 8, 2005, eff. Jan. 1, 2006.]

MD Rules, Rule 5-706, MD R REV Rule 5-706

Current with amendments received through December 1, 2023. Some sections may be more current, see credits for details.

CHAPTER 800
HEARSAY

RULE 5-801

DEFINITIONS

The following definitions apply under this Chapter:

(a) Statement. A "statement" is (1) an oral or written assertion or (2) nonverbal conduct of a person, if it is intended by the person as an assertion.

(b) Declarant. A "declarant" is a person who makes a statement.

(c) Hearsay. "Hearsay" is a statement, other than one made by the declarant while testifying at the trial or hearing, offered in evidence to prove the truth of the matter asserted.

◆ ◆ ◆

Committee note: This Rule does not attempt to define "assertion," a concept best left to development in the case law. The fact that proffered evidence is in the form of a question or something other than a narrative statement, however, does not necessarily preclude its being an assertion. The Rule also does not attempt to define when an assertion, such as a verbal act, is offered for something other than its truth.

Source: This Rule is derived from F.R.Ev. 801(a), (b), and (c).

Credits

[Adopted Dec. 15, 1993, eff. July 1, 1994.]

MD Rules, Rule 5-801, MD R REV Rule 5-801

Current with amendments received through December 1, 2023. Some sections may be more current, see credits for details.

RULE 5-802

HEARSAY RULE

Effective: July 1, 2023

Except as otherwise provided by these rules or permitted by applicable constitutional provisions or statutes, hearsay is not admissible.

♦ ♦ ♦

Cross reference: For an example of a statute permitting the admission of hearsay, see Code, Criminal Procedure Article, § 11-304 concerning the admissibility of an out-of-court statement by a child victim or witness under certain circumstances.

Source: This Rule is derived from F.R.Ev. 802.

Credits

[Adopted Dec. 15, 1993, eff. July 1, 1994. Amended April 1, 2023, eff. July 1, 2023.]

MD Rules, Rule 5-802, MD R REV Rule 5-802

Current with amendments received through December 1, 2023. Some sections may be more current, see credits for details.

RULE 5-802.1

HEARSAY EXCEPTIONS—
PRIOR STATEMENTS BY WITNESSES

The following statements previously made by a witness who testifies at the trial or hearing and who is subject to cross-examination concerning the statement are not excluded by the hearsay rule:

(a) A statement that is inconsistent with the declarant's testimony, if the statement was (1) given under oath subject to the penalty of perjury at a trial, hearing, or other proceeding or in a deposition; (2) reduced to writing and was signed by the declarant; or (3) recorded in substantially verbatim fashion by stenographic or electronic means contemporaneously with the making of the statement;

(b) A statement that is consistent with the declarant's testimony, if the statement is offered to rebut an express or implied charge against the declarant of fabrication, or improper influence or motive;

(c) A statement that is one of identification of a person made after perceiving the person;

(d) A statement that is one of prompt complaint of sexually assaultive behavior to which the declarant was subjected if the statement is consistent with the declarant's testimony; or

(e) A statement that is in the form of a memorandum or record concerning a matter about which the witness once had knowledge but now has insufficient recollection to enable the witness to testify fully and accurately, if the statement was made or adopted by the witness when the matter was fresh in the witness's memory and reflects that knowledge correctly. If admitted, the statement may be read into evidence but the memorandum or record may not itself be received as an exhibit unless offered by an adverse party.

◆ ◆ ◆

Cross reference: Rules 2-521 and 4-326.

Committee note: This Rule does not affect the admissibility of prior inconsistent statements for impeachment purposes. A memorandum or record that is not received as an exhibit under section (e) of this Rule should be marked for identification.

Source: Section (a) of this Rule is derived from Hawaii R.Ev. 802.1(1). Sections (b) and (c) are derived from F.R.Ev. 801(d)(1)(B) and (C). Section (d) is new. Section (e) is derived without substantive change from F.R.Ev. 803(5). Any language differences are solely for purposes of style and clarification.

Credits

[Adopted Dec. 15, 1993, eff. July 1, 1994. Amended Nov. 8, 2005, eff. Jan. 1, 2006.]

MD Rules, Rule 5-802.1, MD R REV Rule 5-802.1

Current with amendments received through December 1, 2023. Some sections may be more current, see credits for details.

RULE 5-803

HEARSAY EXCEPTIONS: UNAVAILABILITY OF DECLARANT NOT REQUIRED

Effective: October 1, 2021

The following are not excluded by the hearsay rule, even though the declarant is available as a witness:

(a) Statement by Party-Opponent. A statement that is offered against a party and is:

(1) The party's own statement, in either an individual or representative capacity;

(2) A statement of which the party has manifested an adoption or belief in its truth;

(3) A statement by a person authorized by the party to make a statement concerning the subject;

(4) A statement by the party's agent or employee made during the agency or employment relationship concerning a matter within the scope of the agency or employment; or

(5) A statement by a coconspirator of the party during the course and in furtherance of the conspiracy.

◆ ◆ ◆

Committee note: Where there is a disputed issue as to scope of employment, representative capacity, authorization to make a statement, the existence of a conspiracy, or any other foundational requirement, the court must make a finding on that issue before the statement may be admitted. These rules do not address whether the court may consider the statement itself in making that determination. Compare *Daugherty v. Kessler*, 264 Md. 281, 291-92 (1972) (civil conspiracy); and *Hlista v. Altevogt*, 239 Md. 43, 51 (1965) (employment relationship) with *Bourjaily v. United States*, 483 U.S. 171, 107 S.Ct. 775 (1987) (trial court may consider the out-of-court statement in deciding whether foundational requirements for coconspirator exception have been met.)

♦ ♦ ♦

(b) Other Exceptions.

(1) *Present Sense Impression.* A statement describing or explaining an event or condition made while the declarant was perceiving the event or condition, or immediately thereafter.

(2) *Excited Utterance.* A statement relating to a startling event or condition made while the declarant was under the stress of excitement caused by the event or condition.

(3) *Then Existing Mental, Emotional, or Physical Condition.* A statement of the declarant's then existing state of mind, emotion, sensation, or physical condition (such as intent, plan, motive, design, mental feeling, pain, and bodily health), offered to prove the declarant's then existing condition or the declarant's future action, but not including a statement of memory or belief to prove the fact remembered or believed unless it relates to the execution, revocation, identification, or terms of declarant's will.

(4) *Statements for Purposes of Medical Diagnosis or Treatment.* Statements made for purposes of medical treatment or medical diagnosis in contemplation of treatment and describing medical history, or past or present

symptoms, pain, or sensation, or the inception or general character of the cause or external sources thereof insofar as reasonably pertinent to treatment or diagnosis in contemplation of treatment.

(5) *Recorded Recollection.* See Rule 5-802.1 (e) for recorded recollection.

(6) *Records of Regularly Conducted Business Activity.* A memorandum, report, record, or data compilation of acts, events, conditions, opinions, or diagnoses if (A) it was made at or near the time of the act, event, or condition, or the rendition of the diagnosis, (B) it was made by a person with knowledge or from information transmitted by a person with knowledge, (C) it was made and kept in the course of a regularly conducted business activity, and (D) the regular practice of that business was to make and keep the memorandum, report, record, or data compilation. A record of this kind may be excluded if the source of information or the method or circumstances of the preparation of the record indicate that the information in the record lacks trustworthiness. In this paragraph, "business" includes business, institution, association, profession, occupation, and calling of every kind, whether or not conducted for profit.

◆ ◆ ◆

Cross reference: Rule 5-902 (12).

Committee note: Public records specifically excluded from the public records exceptions in subsection (b)(8) of this Rule may not be admitted pursuant to this exception.

◆ ◆ ◆

(7) *Absence of Entry in Records Kept in Accordance With Subsection (b)(6).* Unless the circumstances indicate a lack of trustworthiness, evidence that a diligent search disclosed that a matter is not included in the memoranda, reports, records, or data compilations kept in accordance with subsection (b)(6), when offered to prove the nonoccurrence or nonexistence of the matter, if the matter was of a kind about which a memorandum, report, record, or data compilation was regularly made and preserved.

(8) *Public Records and Reports.*

(A) Except as otherwise provided in this paragraph, a memorandum, report, record, statement, or data compilation made by a public agency setting forth

(i) the activities of the agency;

(ii) matters observed pursuant to a duty imposed by law, as to which matters there was a duty to report;

(iii) in civil actions and when offered against the State in criminal actions, factual findings resulting from an investigation made pursuant to authority granted by law; or

(iv) in a final protective order hearing conducted pursuant to Code, Family Law Article, § 4-506, factual findings reported to a court pursuant to Code, Family Law Article, § 4-505, provided that the parties have had a fair opportunity to review the report.

♦ ♦ ♦

Committee note: If necessary, a continuance of a final protective order hearing may be granted in order to provide the parties a fair opportunity to review the report and to prepare for the hearing.

♦ ♦ ♦

(B) A record offered pursuant to paragraph (A) may be excluded if the source of information or the method or circumstance of the preparation of the record indicate that the record or the information in the record lacks trustworthiness.

(C) Except as provided in subsection (b)(8)(D) of this Rule, a record of matters observed by a law enforcement person is not admissible under this paragraph when offered against an accused in a criminal action.

(D) Subject to Rule 5-805, an electronic recording of a matter made by a body camera worn by a law enforcement person or by another type of recording device employed by a law enforcement agency may be admitted when offered against an accused if (i) it is properly authenticated, (ii) it was made contemporaneously with the matter recorded, and (iii) circumstances do not indicate a lack of trustworthiness.

♦ ♦ ♦

Committee note: Subsection (b)(8)(D) establishes requirements for the admission of certain electronic recordings made by a body camera worn by a law enforcement person or by another type of recording device employed by a law enforcement agency against an accused. Subsection (b)(8)(D) does not preclude an accused from offering on his or her own behalf a record of matters observed by a law enforcement person, including a recording made by a body camera. This section does not mandate following the interpretation of the term "factual findings" set forth in *Beech Aircraft Corp. v. Rainey*, 488 U.S. 153 (1988). See *Ellsworth v. Sherne Lingerie, Inc.*, 303 Md. 581 (1985).

♦ ♦ ♦

(9) *Records of Vital Statistics.* Except as otherwise provided by statute, records or data compilations of births, fetal deaths, deaths, or marriages, if the report thereof was made to a public office pursuant to requirements of law.

♦ ♦ ♦

Cross reference: See Code, Health General Article, § 4-223 (inadmissibility of certain information when paternity is contested) and § 5-311 (admissibility of medical examiner's reports).

♦ ♦ ♦

(10) *Absence of Public Record or Entry.* Unless the circumstances indicate a lack of trustworthiness, evidence in the form of testimony or a certification in accordance with Rule 5-902 that a diligent search has failed to disclose a record, report, statement, or data compilation made by a public agency, or an entry therein, when offered to prove the absence of such a record or entry or the nonoccurrence or non-existence of a matter about which a record was regularly made and preserved by the public agency.

(11) *Records of Religious Organizations.* Statements of births, marriages, divorces, deaths, legitimacy, ancestry, relationship by blood or marriage, or other similar facts of personal or family history, contained in a regularly kept record of a religious organization.

(12) *Marriage, Baptismal, and Similar Certificates.* Statements of fact contained in a certificate that the maker performed a marriage or other ceremony or administered a sacrament, made by a member of the clergy, public official, or other person authorized by the rules or practices of a religious organization

or by law to perform the act certified, and purporting to have been issued at the time of the act or within a reasonable time thereafter.

(13) *Family Records.* Statements of fact concerning personal or family history contained in family Bibles, genealogies, charts, engravings on rings, inscriptions on family portraits, engravings on urns, crypts, or tombstones or the like.

(14) *Records of Documents Affecting an Interest in Property.* The record of a document purporting to establish or affect an interest in property, as proof of the content of the original recorded document and its execution and delivery by each person by whom it purports to have been executed, if the record is a record of a public office and a statute authorizes the recording of documents of that kind in that office.

(15) *Statements in Documents Affecting an Interest in Property.* A statement contained in a document purporting to establish or affect an interest in property if the matter stated was relevant to the purpose of the document, unless dealings with the property since the document was made have been inconsistent with the truth of the statement or the purport of the document or the circumstances otherwise indicate lack of trustworthiness.

(16) *Statements in Ancient Documents.* Statements in a document in existence twenty years or more, the authenticity of which is established, unless the circumstances indicate lack of trustworthiness.

(17) *Market Reports and Published Compilations.* Market quotations, tabulations, lists, directories, and other published compilations, generally used and reasonably relied upon by the public or by persons in particular occupations.

(18) *Learned Treatises.* To the extent called to the attention of an expert witness upon cross-examination or relied upon by the expert witness in direct examination, statements contained in a published treatise, periodical, or pamphlet on a subject of history, medicine, or other science or art, established as a reliable authority by the testimony or admission of the witness, by other expert testimony, or by judicial notice. If admitted, the statements may be read into evidence but may not be received as exhibits.

(19) *Reputation Concerning Personal or Family History.* Reputation, prior to the controversy before the court, among members of a person's family by blood, adoption, or marriage, or among a person's associates, or in the community, concerning a person's birth,

adoption, marriage, divorce, death, or other similar fact of personal or family history.

(20) *Reputation Concerning Boundaries or General History.*

    (A) Reputation in a community, prior to the controversy before the court, as to boundaries of, interests in, or customs affecting lands in the community.

    (B) Reputation as to events of general history important to the community, state, or nation where the historical events occurred.

(21) *Reputation as to Character.* Reputation of a person's character among associates or in the community.

(22) *[Vacant].* There is no subsection 22.

(23) *Judgment as to Personal, Family, or General History, or Boundaries.* Judgments as proof of matters of personal, family, or general history, or boundaries, essential to the judgment, if the matter would be provable by evidence of reputation under subsections (19) or (20).

(24) *Other Exceptions.* Under exceptional circumstances, the following are not excluded by the hearsay rule: A statement not specifically covered by any of the hearsay exceptions listed in this Rule or in Rule 5-804, but having equivalent circumstantial guarantees

of trustworthiness, if the court determines that (A) the statement is offered as evidence of a material fact; (B) the statement is more probative on the point for which it is offered than any other evidence which the proponent can procure through reasonable efforts; and (C) the general purposes of these rules and the interests of justice will best be served by admission of the statement into evidence. A statement may not be admitted under this exception unless the proponent of it makes known to the adverse party, sufficiently in advance of the trial or hearing to provide the adverse party with a fair opportunity to prepare to meet it, the intention to offer the statement and the particulars of it, including the name and address of the declarant.

♦ ♦ ♦

Committee note: The residual exception provided by Rule 5-803 (b)(24) does not contemplate an unfettered exercise of judicial discretion, but it does provide for treating new and presently unanticipated situations which demonstrate a trustworthiness within the spirit of the specifically stated exceptions. Within this framework, room is left for growth and development of the law of evidence in the hearsay area, consistently with the broad purposes expressed in Rule 5-102.

It is intended that the residual hearsay exception will be used very rarely, and only in exceptional circumstances. The Committee does not intend to establish a broad license for trial judges to admit hearsay statements that do not fall within one of the other exceptions contained in Rules 5-803 and 5-804 (b). The residual exception is not meant to authorize major judicial revisions of the hearsay rule, including its present exceptions. Such major revisions are best accomplished by amendments to the Rule itself. It is intended that in any case in which evidence is sought to be admitted under this subsection, the trial judge will exercise no less care, reflection, and caution than the courts did under the common law in establishing the now-recognized exceptions to the hearsay rule.

Source: This Rule is derived as follows:

Section (a) is derived from F.R.Ev. 801(d)(2).

Section (b) is derived from F.R.Ev. 803.

Credits

[Adopted Dec. 15, 1993, eff. July 1, 1994. Amended Nov. 8, 2005, eff. Jan. 1, 2006; Dec. 4, 2007, eff. Jan. 1, 2008; Sept. 17, 2015, eff. Jan. 1, 2016; Dec. 13, 2016, eff. Apr. 1, 2017; July 9, 2021, eff. Oct. 1, 2021.]

MD Rules, Rule 5-803, MD R REV Rule 5-803

Current with amendments received through December 1, 2023. Some sections may be more current, see credits for details.

RULE 5-804

HEARSAY EXCEPTIONS; DECLARANT UNAVAILABLE

(a) Definition of Unavailability. "Unavailability as a witness" includes situations in which the declarant:

(1)   is exempted by ruling of the court on the ground of privilege from testifying concerning the subject matter of the declarant's statement;

(2)   refuses to testify concerning the subject matter of the declarant's statement despite an order of the court to do so;

(3)   testifies to a lack of memory of the subject matter of the declarant's statement;

(4)   is unable to be present or to testify at the hearing because of death or then existing physical or mental illness or infirmity; or

(5)   is absent from the hearing and the proponent of the statement has been unable to procure the declarant's attendance (or in the case of a hearsay exception under subsection (b)(2), (3), or (4) of this Rule, the declarant's attendance or testimony) by process or other reasonable means.

A statement will not qualify under section (b) of this Rule if the unavailability is due to the procurement or wrongdoing of the proponent of the statement for the purpose of preventing the witness from attending or testifying.

(b) Hearsay Exceptions. The following are not excluded by the hearsay rule if the declarant is unavailable as a witness:

(1) *Former Testimony.* Testimony given as a witness in any action or proceeding or in a deposition taken in compliance with law in the course of any action or proceeding, if the party against whom the testimony is now offered, or, in a civil action or proceeding, a predecessor in interest, had an opportunity and similar motive to develop the testimony by direct, cross, or redirect examination.

(2) *Statement Under Belief of Impending Death.* In a prosecution for an offense based upon an unlawful homicide, attempted homicide, or assault with intent to commit a homicide or in any civil action, a statement made by a declarant, while believing that the declarant's death was imminent, concerning the cause or circumstances of what the declarant believed to be his or her impending death.

(3) *Statement Against Interest.* A statement which was at the time of its making so contrary to the declarant's pecuniary or proprietary interest, so tended to subject the declarant to civil or criminal liability, or so tended to render invalid a claim by the declarant against another, that a reasonable person in the declarant's position would not have made

the statement unless the person believed it to be true. A statement tending to expose the declarant to criminal liability and offered in a criminal case is not admissible unless corroborating circumstances clearly indicate the trustworthiness of the statement.

♦ ♦ ♦

Cross reference: See Code, Courts Article, § 10-920, distinguishing expressions of regret or apology by health care providers from admissions of liability or fault.

♦ ♦ ♦

(4) *Statement of Personal or Family History.*

(A) A statement concerning the declarant's own birth; adoption; marriage; divorce; legitimacy; ancestry; relationship by blood, adoption, or marriage; or other similar fact of personal or family history, even though the declarant had no means of acquiring personal knowledge of the matter stated.

(B) A statement concerning the death of, or any of the facts listed in subsection (4)(A) about another person, if the declarant was related to the other person by blood, adoption, or marriage or was so intimately associated with the other person's family as to be likely to have accurate information concerning the matter declared.

(5)   *Witness Unavailable Because of Party's Wrongdoing.*

(A) Civil Actions. In civil actions in which a witness is unavailable because of a party's wrongdoing, a statement that (i) was (a) given under oath subject to the penalty of perjury at a trial, hearing, or other proceeding or in a deposition; (b) reduced to writing and was signed by the declarant; or (c) recorded in substantially verbatim fashion by stenographic or electronic means contemporaneously with the making of the statement, and (ii) is offered against a party who has engaged in, directed, or conspired to commit wrongdoing that was intended to, and did, procure the unavailability of the declarant as a witness, provided however the statement may not be admitted unless, as soon as practicable after the proponent of the statement learns that the declarant will be unavailable, the proponent makes known to the adverse party the intention to offer the statement and the particulars of it.

◆   ◆   ◆

Committee note: A "party" referred to in subsection (b)(5)(A) also includes an agent of the government.

◆   ◆   ◆

(B) Criminal Causes. In criminal causes in which a witness is unavailable because of a party's wrongdoing, admission of the witness's statement under this exception is governed by Code, Courts Article, § 10-901.

♦ ♦ ♦

Committee note: Subsection (b)(5) of this Rule does not affect the law of spoliation, "guilty knowledge," or unexplained failure to produce a witness to whom one has superior access. See *Washington v. State*, 293 Md. 465, 468 n. 1 (1982); *Breeding v. State*, 220 Md. 193, 197 (1959); *Shpak v. Schertle*, 97 Md. App. 207, 222-27 (1993); *Meyer v. McDonnell*, 40 Md. App. 524, 533, (1978), rev'd on other grounds, 301 Md. 426 (1984); *Larsen v. Romeo*, 254 Md. 220, 228 (1969); *Hoverter v. Director of Patuxent Inst.*, 231 Md. 608, 609 (1963); and *DiLeo v. Nugent*, 88 Md. App. 59, 69-72 (1991). The hearsay exception set forth in subsection (b)(5) (B) is not available in criminal causes other than those listed in Code, Courts Article, § 10-901 (a).

Cross reference: For the residual hearsay exception applicable regardless of the availability of the declarant, see Rule 5-803 (b)(24).

Source: This Rule is derived from F.R.Ev. 804.

Credits

[Adopted Dec. 15, 1993, eff. July 1, 1994. Amended Nov. 8, 2005, eff. Jan. 1, 2006; June 16, 2009, eff. June 17, 2009; Oct. 20, 2010, eff. Jan. 1, 2011.]

MD Rules, Rule 5-804, MD R REV Rule 5-804

Current with amendments received through December 1, 2023. Some sections may be more current, see credits for details.

RULE 5-805

HEARSAY WITHIN HEARSAY

If one or more hearsay statements are contained within another hearsay statement, each must fall within an exception to the hearsay rule in order not to be excluded by that rule.

♦ ♦ ♦

Source: This Rule is derived without substantive change from F.R.Ev. 805. Any language differences are solely for purposes of style and clarification.

Credits

[Adopted Dec. 15, 1993, eff. July 1, 1994.]

MD Rules, Rule 5-805, MD R REV Rule 5-805

Current with amendments received through December 1, 2023. Some sections may be more current, see credits for details.

RULE 5-806

ATTACKING AND SUPPORTING CREDIBILITY OF DECLARANT

(a) In General. When a hearsay statement has been admitted in evidence, the credibility of the declarant may be attacked, and if attacked may be supported, by any evidence which would be admissible for those purposes if the declarant had testified as a witness. Evidence of a statement or conduct by the declarant at any time, inconsistent with the declarant's hearsay statement, is not subject to any requirement that the declarant may have been afforded an opportunity to deny or explain. If the party against whom a hearsay statement has been admitted calls the declarant as a witness, the party is entitled to examine the declarant on the statement as if under cross-examination.

(b) Exception. This Rule does not apply to statements by party-opponents under Rule 5-803(a)(1) and (a)(2).

♦ ♦ ♦

Source: This Rule is derived from F.R.Ev. 806.

Credits

[Adopted Dec. 15, 1993, eff. July 1, 1994.]

MD Rules, Rule 5-806, MD R REV Rule 5-806

Current with amendments received through December 1, 2023. Some sections may be more current, see credits for details.

CHAPTER 900
AUTHENTICATION AND IDENTIFICATION

RULE 5-901

REQUIREMENT OF AUTHENTICATION
OR IDENTIFICATION

Effective: October 1, 2021

(a) General Provision. The requirement of authentication or identification as a condition precedent to admissibility is satisfied by evidence sufficient to support a finding that the matter in question is what its proponent claims.

Cross reference: Rule 5-104(b).

(b) Illustrations. By way of illustration only, and not by way of limitation, the following are examples of authentication or identification conforming with the requirements of this Rule:

(1) *Testimony of Witness With Knowledge.* Testimony of a witness with knowledge that the offered evidence is what it is claimed to be.

(2) *Non-Expert Opinion on Handwriting.* Non-expert opinion as to the genuineness of handwriting, based upon familiarity not acquired for purposes of the litigation.

(3) *Comparison With Authenticated Specimens.* Comparison by the court or an expert witness with specimens that have been authenticated.

(4) *Circumstantial Evidence.* Circumstantial evidence, such as appearance, contents, substance, internal patterns, location, or other distinctive characteristics, that the offered evidence is what it is claimed to be.

(5) *Voice Identification.* Identification of a voice, whether heard firsthand or through mechanical or electronic transmission or recording, based upon the witness having heard the voice at any time under circumstances connecting it with the alleged speaker.

(6) *Telephone Conversation.* A telephone conversation, by evidence that a telephone call

was made to the number assigned at the time to a particular person or business, if

(A) in the case of a person, circumstances, including self-identification, show the person answering to be the one called, or

(B) in the case of a business, the call was made to a place of business and the conversation related to business reasonably transacted over the telephone.

(7) *Public Record.* Evidence that a writing authorized by law to be recorded or filed and in fact recorded or filed in a public office, or a purported public record, report, statement, or data compilation, is from the public office where items of this nature are kept.

(8) *Ancient Document or Data Compilation.* Evidence that a document or data compilation:

(A) is in such condition as to create no suspicion concerning its authenticity,

(B) was in a place where, if authentic, it would likely be, and

(C) has been in existence twenty years or more at the time it is offered.

(9) *Process or System.* Evidence describing a process or system used to produce the proffered exhibit or testimony and showing that the process or system produces an accurate result.

◆ ◆ ◆

Committee note: This Rule is not intended to indicate the type of evidence that may be required to establish that a system or process produces an accurate result. See, e.g., Rule 5-702.

♦ ♦ ♦

(10) *Methods Provided by Statute or Rule.* Any method of authentication or identification provided by statute or by these rules.

♦ ♦ ♦

Cross reference: Code, Courts Article, § 10-104, § 10-105, and §§ 10-1001 through 10-1004.

Source: This Rule is derived from F.R.Ev. 901.

Credits

[Adopted Dec. 15, 1993, eff. July 1, 1994. Amended Feb. 10, 1998, eff. July 1, 1998; July 9, 2021, eff. Oct. 1, 2021.]

MD Rules, Rule 5-901, MD R REV Rule 5-901

Current with amendments received through December 1, 2023. Some sections may be more current, see credits for details.

RULE 5-902

SELF-AUTHENTICATION

Effective: October 1, 2021

Subject to the conditions in this Rule, the following items of evidence are self-authenticating, and, except as required by statute or this Rule, require no testimony or other extrinsic evidence of authenticity in order to be admitted:

(1) **Domestic Public Documents Under Seal.** A document bearing a seal purporting to be that of the
United States, or of any state, district, common-
wealth, territory, or insular possession thereof,
or the Panama Canal Zone, or the trust territory
of the Pacific Islands, or of a political subdivision, department, officer, or agency thereof, and
a signature purporting to be an attestation or
execution.

(2) **Domestic Public Documents Not Under Seal.** A
document purporting to bear the signature in the
official capacity of an officer or employee of any
entity included in paragraph (1) of this Rule, having no seal, if a public officer having a seal and
having official duties in the district or political
subdivision of the officer or employee certifies
under seal that the signer has the official capacity
and that the signature is genuine.

(3) **Foreign Public Documents.** A document that
purports to be signed or attested by a person who
is authorized by a foreign country's law to do so.
The document must be accompanied by a final
certification that certifies the genuineness of the
signature and official position of the signer or
attester—or of any foreign official whose certificate of genuineness relates to the signature
or attestation or is in a chain of certificates of
genuineness relating to the signature or attestation. The certification may be made by a secre-
tary of a United States embassy or legation; by a

consul general, vice consul, or consular agent of the United States; or by a diplomatic or consular official of the foreign country assigned or accredited to the United States. If all parties have been given a reasonable opportunity to investigate the document's authenticity and accuracy, the court may, for good cause, either:

(A)   order that it be treated as presumptively authentic without final certification; or

(B)   allow it to be evidenced by an attested summary with or without final certification.

(4)   Certified Copies of Public Records. A copy of an official record or report or entry therein, or of a document authorized by law to be recorded or filed and actually recorded or filed in a public office, including data compilations, certified as correct by the custodian or other person authorized to make the certification, by certificate complying with this Rule or complying with any applicable statute or these rules.

(5)   Official Publications. Books, pamphlets, or other publications purporting to be issued or authorized by a public agency.

(6)   Newspapers and Periodicals. Printed materials purporting to be newspapers or periodicals.

(7)   Trade Inscriptions and the Like. Inscriptions, signs, tags, or labels purporting to have been affixed in the course of business and indicating ownership, control, or origin.

(8) Acknowledged Documents. Documents accompanied by a certificate of acknowledgment executed in the manner provided by law by a notary public or other officer authorized by law to take acknowledgments.

(9) Commercial Paper and Related Documents. To the extent provided by applicable commercial law, commercial paper, signatures thereon, and related documents.

◆ ◆ ◆

Cross reference: See, e.g., Code, Commercial Law Article, §§ 1-202, 3-308, and 3-505.

◆ ◆ ◆

(10) Presumptions Under Statutes or Treaties. Any signature, document, or other matter declared by applicable statute or treaty to be presumptively genuine or authentic.

(11) Items as to Which Required Objections Not Made. Unless justice otherwise requires, any item as to which, by statute, rule, or court order, a written objection as to authenticity is required to be made before trial, and an objection was not made in conformance with the statute, rule, or order.

(12) Certified Records of Regularly Conducted Activity. The original or a copy of a record of a regularly conducted activity that meets the requirements of Rule 5-803 (b)(6)(A)-(D) and has been certified in a Certification of Custodian of Records or Other Qualified Individual Form substantially in compliance with such a form approved by the State Court Administrator and posted on the Judiciary website, provided that, before the trial or hearing in which the record will be offered into evidence, the proponent (A) gives an adverse party reasonable written notice of the intent to offer the record and (B) makes the record and certification available for inspection so that the adverse party has a fair opportunity to challenge them on the ground that the sources of information or the method or circumstances of preparation indicate lack of trustworthiness.

♦ ♦ ♦

Committee note: An objection to self-authentication under paragraph (12) of this Rule made in advance of trial does not constitute a waiver of any other ground that may be asserted as to admissibility at trial.

♦ ♦ ♦

In a consumer debt collection action not resolved by judgment on affidavit, Code, Courts Article, § 5-1203 (b)(2) requires that a debt buyer or a collector acting on behalf of a debt buyer introduce specified documents "in accordance with the Rules of Evidence applicable to actions that are not small claims actions brought under § 4-405 of this Article." Consequently, if the debt buyer or collector intends to offer business records into evidence in a small claim action without in-court testimony of a witness, the debt buyer must provide notice to the opposing party in conformance with Rule 5-902 (12).

(13) Certified Records Generated by an Electronic Process or System. A record generated by an electronic process or system that produces an accurate result, as shown by a certification of a qualified person that complies with the certification and notification requirements of paragraph (12) of this Rule.

(14) Certified Data Copied from an Electronic Device, Storage Medium, or File. Data copied from an electronic device, storage medium, or file, if authenticated by a process of digital identification, as shown by a certification of a qualified person that complies with the certification and notification requirements of paragraph (12) of this Rule.

◆ ◆ ◆

Committee note: Paragraphs 13 and 14 of this Rule are derived from Fed. R. Evid. 902 (13) and (14). See Advisory Committee Notes attached to the federal provisions for an explanation of how these provisions are intended to operate.

Nothing in paragraphs (13) and (14) is intended to limit a party from establishing authenticity of electronic evidence on any ground provided in these Rules, including under Rule 5-901 or through judicial notice where appropriate.

A certification under paragraphs (13) and (14) can only establish that the proffered item is authentic. The opponent remains free to object to admissibility of the proffered item on other grounds.

Source: This Rule is in part derived from the 2020 version of Fed. R. Evid. 902 and is in part new.

Credits

[Adopted Dec. 15, 1993, eff. July 1, 1994. Amended Nov. 8, 2005, eff. Jan. 1, 2006; Dec. 4, 2007, eff. Jan. 1, 2008; Dec. 13, 2016, eff. Apr. 1, 2017; July 9, 2021, eff. Oct. 1, 2021.]

MD Rules, Rule 5-902, MD R REV Rule 5-902

Current with amendments received through December 1, 2023. Some sections may be more current, see credits for details.

RULE 5-903

SUBSCRIBING WITNESS TESTIMONY UNNECESSARY

Except as provided by statute, the testimony of a subscribing witness is not required to authenticate a writing.

♦ ♦ ♦

Cross reference: See Code, Courts Article, § 10-906 concerning the authentication of wills and codicils.

Source: This Rule is derived from F.R.Ev. 903.

Credits

[Adopted Dec. 15, 1993, eff. July 1, 1994.]

MD Rules, Rule 5-903, MD R REV Rule 5-903

Current with amendments received through December 1, 2023. Some sections may be more current, see credits for details.

CHAPTER 1000
CONTENTS OF WRITINGS, RECORDINGS, AND PHOTOGRAPHS

RULE 5-1001

DEFINITIONS

In this Chapter the following definitions apply except as expressly otherwise provided or as necessary implication requires:

(a) Writings and Recordings. "Writings" and "recordings" consist of letters, words, numbers, or their equivalent, set down by handwriting, typewriting, printing, photostating, photographing, magnetic or optical impulse, mechanical or electronic recording, or other form of data compilation.

Committee note: This is not intended to change the common law regarding the court's discretion to treat chattels inscribed with letters or numbers as writings.

(b) Photographs. "Photographs" include still photographs, X-ray films, video tapes, and motion pictures.

(c) Original. An "original" of a writing or recording is the writing or recording itself or any counterpart intended to have the same effect by a person executing or issuing it. An "original" of a photograph includes the negative or any print therefrom. If data are stored in a computer or similar device, any printout or other output readable by sight, shown to reflect the data accurately, is an "original".

(d) Duplicate. A "duplicate" is a counterpart produced by the same impression as the original, or from the same matrix, or by means of photography, including enlargements and miniatures, or by mechanical or electronic re-recordings, or by chemical reproduction, or by other equivalent technique which accurately reproduces the original.

♦ ♦ ♦

Source: This Rule is derived from F.R.Ev. 1001.

Credits

[Adopted Dec. 15, 1993, eff. July 1, 1994.]

MD Rules, Rule 5-1001, MD R REV Rule 5-1001

Current with amendments received through December 1, 2023. Some sections may be more current, see credits for details.

RULE 5-1002

REQUIREMENT OF ORIGINAL

To prove the content of a writing, recording, or photograph, the original writing, recording, or photograph is required, except as otherwise provided in these rules or by statute.

♦ ♦ ♦

Source: This Rule is derived from F.R.Ev. 1002.

Credits

[Adopted Dec. 15, 1993, eff. July 1, 1994.]

MD Rules, Rule 5-1002, MD R REV Rule 5-1002

Current with amendments received through December 1, 2023. Some sections may be more current, see credits for details.

RULE 5-1003

ADMISSIBILITY OF DUPLICATES

A duplicate is admissible to the same extent as an original unless (1) a genuine question is raised as to the authenticity of the original or (2) in the circumstances it would be unfair to admit the duplicate in lieu of the original.

◆ ◆ ◆

Source: This Rule is derived from F.R.Ev. 1003.

Credits

[Adopted Dec. 15, 1993, eff. July 1, 1994.]

MD Rules, Rule 5-1003, MD R REV Rule 5-1003

Current with amendments received through December 1, 2023. Some sections may be more current, see credits for details.

RULE 5-1004

ADMISSIBILITY OF OTHER EVIDENCE OF CONTENTS

The contents of a writing, recording, or photograph may be proved by evidence other than the original if:

(a) Original Lost or Destroyed. All originals are lost or have been destroyed, unless the proponent lost or destroyed them in bad faith;

(b) **Original Not Obtainable.** No original can be obtained by any reasonably practicable, available judicial process or procedure;

(c) **Original in Possession of Opponent.** At a time when an original was under the control of the party against whom offered, that party was put on notice, by the pleadings or otherwise, that the contents would be a subject of proof at the hearing or trial, and that party does not produce the original at the hearing or trial; or

(d) **Collateral Matters.** The writing, recording, or photograph is not closely related to a controlling issue.

◆   ◆   ◆

Cross reference: For admissibility of duplicates, see Rule 5-1003.

Source: This Rule is derived from F.R.Ev. 1004.

Credits

[Adopted Dec. 15, 1993, eff. July 1, 1994.]

MD Rules, Rule 5-1004, MD R REV Rule 5-1004

Current with amendments received through December 1, 2023. Some sections may be more current, see credits for details.

RULE 5-1005

PUBLIC RECORDS

The contents of an official record, or of a document authorized to be recorded or filed and actually recorded or filed, including data compilations, if otherwise admissible, may be proved by copy, certified as correct in accordance with Rule 5-902 or testified to be correct by a witness who has compared it with the original. If a copy that complies with the foregoing cannot be obtained by the exercise of reasonable diligence, other evidence of the contents may be given.

♦ ♦ ♦

Committee note: The applicability of this Rule is not dependent upon the record or document being located in a place that is accessible to the public.

Source: This Rule is derived from F.R.Ev. 1005.

Credits

[Adopted Dec. 15, 1993, eff. July 1, 1994.]

MD Rules, Rule 5-1005, MD R REV Rule 5-1005

Current with amendments received through December 1, 2023. Some sections may be more current, see credits for details.

RULE 5-1006

SUMMARIES

The contents of voluminous writings, recordings, or photographs, otherwise admissible, which cannot conveniently be examined in court may be presented in the form of a chart, calculation, or other summary. The party intending to use such a summary must give timely notice to all parties of the intention to use the summary and shall make the summary and the originals or duplicates from which the summary is compiled available for inspection and copying by other parties at a reasonable time and place. The court may order that they be produced in court.

◆ ◆ ◆

Source: This Rule is derived from F.R.Ev. 1006.

Credits

[Adopted Dec. 15, 1993, eff. July 1, 1994.]

MD Rules, Rule 5-1006, MD R REV Rule 5-1006

Current with amendments received through December 1, 2023. Some sections may be more current, see credits for details.

RULE 5-1007

TESTIMONY OR WRITTEN ADMISSION OF PARTY

Contents of writings, recordings, or photographs may be proved by the testimony or deposition of the party against whom offered or by the party's written admission, without accounting for the nonproduction of the original.

◆ ◆ ◆

Source: This Rule is derived from F.R.Ev. 1007.

Credits

[Adopted Dec. 15, 1993, eff. July 1, 1994.]

MD Rules, Rule 5-1007, MD R REV Rule 5-1007

Current with amendments received through December 1, 2023. Some sections may be more current, see credits for details.

RULE 5-1008

FUNCTIONS OF COURT AND JURY

(a) Generally. Except as otherwise provided in section (b) of this Rule, when the admissibility of evidence other than the original of contents of writings, recordings, or photographs under these rules depends upon the fulfillment of a condition of fact, the question whether the condition has been fulfilled is for the court to determine in accordance with the provisions of Rule 5-104(a).

(b) Exceptions. The following issues, if raised, are for the trier of fact to determine as in the case of other issues of fact: (1) whether the asserted writing, recording, or photograph ever existed, (2) whether another writing, recording, or photograph produced at the trial is the original, or (3) whether evidence of contents other than the original correctly reflects the contents.

◆ ◆ ◆

Source: This Rule is derived from F.R.Ev. 1008.

Credits

[Adopted Dec. 15, 1993, eff. July 1, 1994.]

MD Rules, Rule 5-1008, MD R REV Rule 5-1008

Current with amendments received through December 1, 2023. Some sections may be more current, see credits for details.

www.ingramcontent.com/pod-product-compliance
Lightning Source LLC
Chambersburg PA
CBHW061610220326
41598CB00024BC/3532